Rookie
Read-About® Science

Trees to Paper

by Lisa M. Herrington

Content Consultant
John Williams, President, Maine Pulp & Paper Association

Reading Consultant
Jeanne Clidas, Ph.D.

Children's Press®
An Imprint of Scholastic Inc.
New York Toronto London Auckland Sydney
Mexico City New Delhi Hong Kong
Danbury, Connecticut

Cataloging-in-Publication Data is available from the Library of Congress

ISBN 978-0-531-24744-0 (lib. bdg.)
ISBN 978-0-531-24710-5 (pbk.)

Produced by Spooky Cheetah Press

© 2013 by Scholastic Inc.

All rights reserved. Published in 2013 by Children's Press, an imprint of Scholastic Inc.

Printed in China 62

1 2 3 4 5 6 7 8 9 10 R 22 21 20 19 18 17 16 15 14 13

Photographs © 2013: age fotostock: cover top center, 12, 30 second from top (John Zoi), 15, 30 center top, 31 center bottom (Maurizio Grimaldi); Alamy Images: 20, 30 second from bottom (Dan Lee), 28 (Rob Walls); Dreamstime: cover bottom (Oksix), 4 (Stephanie Swartz); Media Bakery: 16, 31 bottom; Newscom/David R. Frazier/DanitaDelimont.com: cover top right, 11, 19, 23, 24, 30 center bottom, 31 center top; Shutterstock, Inc.: 27, 30 bottom (Algecireño), 31 top (Mirec), 3 top left (Odin M. Eidskrem), 3 bottom (Oksix); Superstock, Inc./Belinda Images: 8, 30 top; Thinkstock/iStockphoto: cover top left, 3 top right, 7.

Table of Contents

Drawing on paper is fun!

Paper Everywhere!

Paper has many uses. We write on it. We draw on it. We use it to wrap gifts! Find out how paper is made.

Paper was invented in China about 2,000 years ago.

From Trees to Pulp

Did you know that paper comes from trees?

Tall pine trees like these can be made into paper.

First, the trees are cut into logs. The logs are loaded onto trucks. Then they are taken to **paper mills**.

A worker loads logs onto a truck.

At the paper mill, a
machine takes the
bark off the trees.

This tree has had
its bark removed.

The logs are made
into small pieces
called wood chips.

Wood chips
are piled high
at a paper mill.

A large vat of pulp gets ready to be turned into paper.

Water and other things are added to the wood. They become a wet mix. It is called **pulp**.

FUN FACT!

Dye can be added to the pulp to make colored paper.

These students are collecting paper to be recycled.

Pulp can also be made from **recycled** paper. When we recycle, we take something old and use it again.

The screen can move as fast as a car travels on the highway!

From Pulp to Paper

The pulp is ready to become paper. It is sprayed onto a big screen.

FUN FACT!

Some machines can make more than 5,000 feet (1,500 meters) of paper in one minute. That's three times as tall as the tallest skyscraper in the United States!

As the screen moves, the water falls off. The pulp sticks together.

Water is collected under the screen so it can be used again.

The paper is pressed through hot rollers to dry.

The paper is heated and then cooled as it passes through the rollers.

Then the finished paper is wound into huge rolls.

Imagine how long it would take to cover all of this paper with drawings!

The machine's sharp blades slice through a stack of paper.

So Many Choices

Machines cut the paper into many sizes.

FUN FACT!

Americans use about 71 million tons (64 million tonnes) of paper products each year. That equals the weight of almost 5 million school buses!

Paper products come in many shapes, sizes, and colors!

There are many different kinds of paper. They include construction paper, newspaper—even paper bags! How many types can you spot around your home?

FUN FACT!

Thousands of things can be made from recycled paper. They include paper towels, masking tape, lampshades, and egg cartons.

Making Paper
Step by Step

1. Trees are cut into logs.

2. The logs become small pieces called wood chips.

3. The wood is made into wet pulp.

4. The pulp is put on a big screen. As it moves, the water falls off.

5. The damp paper goes through hot rollers.

6. Once dry, the paper is cut.

Glossary

bark (bark): the hard covering on the outside of a tree

paper mills (PAY-pur mils): factories where paper is made

pulp (puhlp): a soft, wet mix of wood and other things

recycled (ree-SYE-kuhld): waste that is turned into something that can be used again

Index

Facts for Now

Visit this Scholastic Web site for more information on how paper is made:
www.factsfornow.scholastic.com
Enter the keyword **Paper**

About the Author

Lisa M. Herrington writes books and magazine articles for kids. She lives in Trumbull, Connecticut, with her family. She loves to doodle and draw on paper with her daughter, Caroline.